MW00668872

YOUNG DARK EMU

A TRUER HISTORY • BRUCE PASCOE

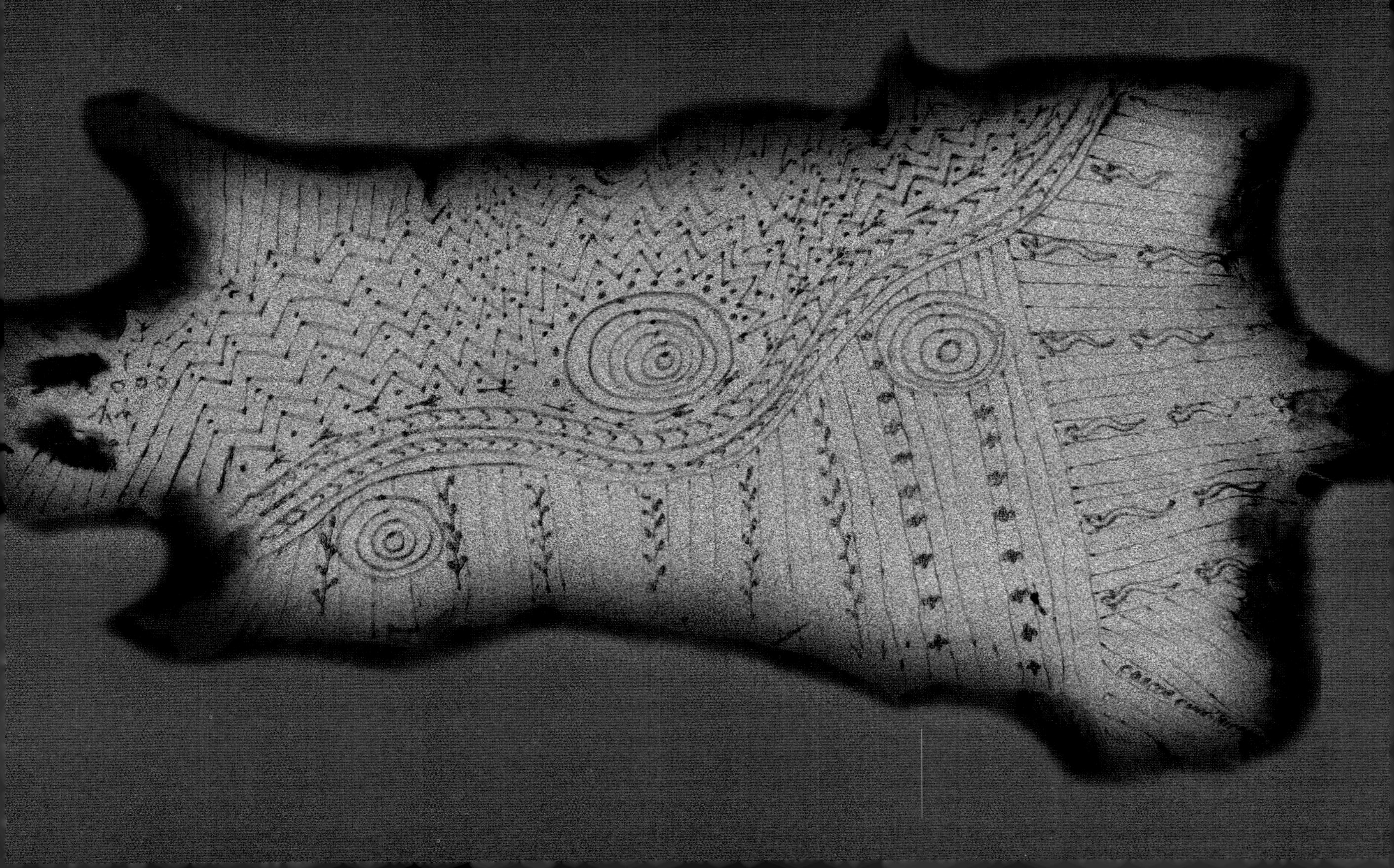

POSSUM SKIN

To the Australians

First published 2019, reprinted twice in 2019, 2021
Magabala Books Aboriginal Corporation,
Broome, Western Australia
Website: www.magabala.com
Email: sales@magabala.com

Magabala Books receives financial assistance from
the Commonwealth Government through the Australia Council,
its arts advisory body.

The State of Western Australia has made an investment in this project
through the Department of Local Government, Sport and Cultural Industries.

Magabala Books would like to acknowledge the generous
support of the Shire of Broome, Western Australia.

Magabala Books acknowledges the support of private donors through
the Magabala Books Cultural Fund, in particular the
Jon & Caro Stewart Family Foundation and Mr David Dureau.

978-1-925360-84-4

A catalogue record for this
book is available from the
National Library of Australia

Packaged by Ballantyne Rawlins in collaboration with Magabala Books
Printed in China by Toppan Leefung Printing Ltd

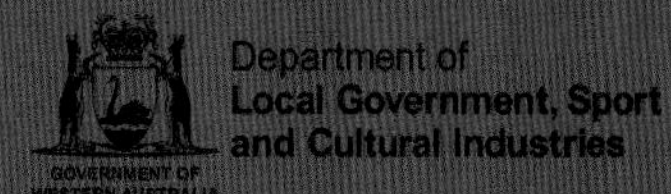

CONTENTS

THROUGHOUT HISTORY, humans have looked to the night sky to help explain their existence, but the conclusions peoples draw from the same sky can be remarkably different. European astronomy uses constellations of stars to tell a story, but sometimes Aboriginal Australia uses the darkness between the stars. Dark Emu is a shape in the dark areas between the stars of the Milky Way.

It's a different way of seeing.

NOTE TO READERS

YOUNG DARK EMU is taken from the book *Dark Emu,* written for older readers. It includes many quotes from people in the past. At times words are used to describe Aboriginal people that are now considered inappropriate.

Young Dark Emu includes extracts from many original nineteenth-century colonial diaries. Because of this, spellings vary between quoted documents.

OPPOSITE: EMU DREAMING. DETAIL OF THE SHAPE BETWEEN THE STARS

INTRODUCTION

WHEN THE BRITISH officers and convicts of the First Fleet arrived in Australia in 1788, their aim was to claim the land as their own.

They considered it their duty to expand the British Empire. They were confident in their assumption that they had the 'right' to occupy the 'empty land'.

It is clear from the journals of early settlers and explorers that few came to Australia to marvel at a new civilisation – they had come to replace it. They planned to clear land, grow crops, farm, build houses, make towns and cities, and establish law and order as they recognised it. In their rush for possession of land, they turned their eyes away from the obvious signs of the civilisation that already existed.

As European explorers and settlers moved across Australia in search of land to claim, they made records and kept diaries, and drew and painted what they saw. These journals and drawings have been the basis for the accepted view of Australia's history. However, when we look at these records carefully, we can see Australia as it was prior to colonisation. The journals show that, for many thousands of years, Aboriginal people had been

working together across the country to farm and care for the land.

It was a very inconvenient truth that Indigenous Australians lived in permanent structures and in large communities, built dams and wells, planted and irrigated and harvested seed, and preserved and stored the surplus. In fact, Aboriginal people had been shaping their land for thousands of years.

None of this fits with the long-held view that Aboriginal Australians lived a roaming nomadic life as hunter-gatherers, surviving day to day solely by collecting fruits and seeds and hunting animals.

In *Young Dark Emu – A Truer History,* I give examples of firsthand accounts, including diaries and illustrations, from early settlers and explorers. These are only a few of the many descriptions in these diaries. And we can only imagine the other Aboriginal villages and farmlands and enterprises across this vast continent that were never recorded.

These eyewitness accounts tell us how Aboriginal people lived and ask you to consider a different view of how Australia was before the British arrived.

They offer a truer history.

ABOVE: FROM THE SKETCHBOOK *SCENES FROM ABORIGINAL LIFE* BY KWAT KWAT ARTIST TOMMY MCRAE, 1862

ONE THE LAND GRAB

ONCE THEIR SENTENCE had been served, many convicts chose to remain in the colony and acquire land. Owning land was something they could never have done if they had returned to England.

In the new colony, administrators and soldiers made themselves rich by buying and selling land. When free settlers began to arrive, they too were greedy for land and quickly acquired any that was available. With all available government land allocated, the newcomers turned to outlying districts beyond the ranges and coves of Sydney. They took with them plenty of weapons and men to use them.

In the earliest days of the colony, Aboriginal people tried to draw the British into the codes of behaviour they expected from 'visitors'. But the colonisers had no intention of respecting Aboriginal law and wholesale war broke out.

The colonisers forcibly drove Aboriginal people from the land, killing thousands in the process in fierce and bloody battles. Aboriginal people could not fall back into neighbouring lands as they had been born to live on, and protect, only the land of their birth – their Country. Initially Aboriginal people fought back against the settlers. There is evidence of battles across the continent

OPPOSITE: DETAIL, JOHN BATMAN'S TREATY WITH THE WURUNDJERI, 1835

Know all Persons that We Three Brothers Jagajaga
Bungarie Yanyan Moowhip
being the Chiefs of a certain Native Tribe called
the above mentioned Chiefs Iramoo being possessed of the Tract of Land herein
Tomahawks One Hundred Knives Fifty Pair of Scissors Thirty Looking G
Flour & Handkfs delivered to Us by John Batman residing in Van Diemens Land
and Successors Give Grant Enfeoff and confirm unto the said John Batman his
hundred from the ... about 7 miles from the
Forty miles across Iramoo Downs or Plains and from thence South
same hath been before the execution of these presents delineated and marked out by Us
along the boundaries of the said Tract of Land To Hold the said Tract of Land
his heirs and Assigns for ever To the Intent that the said John Batman his
thereon Sheep and Cattle Yielding and delivering to Us and our heirs or succ
Blankets One Hundred Tomahawks Fifty Suits of Clothing Fifty Looking Glasses
Jagajaga the before mentioned Principal Chiefs and Cooloolock Bungarie Yanyan Moowhip and
these presents and have signed the same Dated according to the Christian Era this

Signed Sealed and Delivered in the presence of Us the same having been properly interpreted and explained to the said Chiefs

James Gumm

Alexander Thomson

Willm Todd

including on the plains near Robinvale on the Murray River, on the Crawford River in western Victoria, Oyster Bay in Tasmania, Geraldton in Western Australia, the Pascoe River in Queensland, the Hawkesbury in New South Wales and thousands of other locations. However, their fight for their Country could not be maintained. Once defeated, the Aboriginal people remained within their old clan boundaries, but there they were at the mercy of the colonists who had stolen their land.

Many people died in battles and more succumbed to the waves of diseases brought to Australia by the British. Aboriginal people had no resistance to diseases they had not previously been exposed to. It is estimated that some Aboriginal clans lost 80 per cent of their numbers to smallpox alone.

Added to this, Aboriginal people were also starving. The newcomers destroyed indigenous croplands so quickly that Aboriginal people were forced to depend on British food. The combination of deaths from fighting, disease and starvation crushed the Aboriginal resistance. Aboriginal people didn't enter the tiny missions and reserves set aside for them so they could become civilised; they entered because they were starving and had no choice.

OPPOSITE: CONFLICT ON THE RUFUS. PUBLISHED IN *THE ILLUSTRATED MELBOURNE POST*, 1866

ABOVE: FROM THE SKETCHBOOK *SCENES FROM ABORIGINAL LIFE* BY KWAT KWAT ARTIST TOMMY MCRAE, 1862

During the war between Aboriginal people and British settlers, the government made token gestures to stop the land grab. However, after several British men were hanged for the massacre of Aboriginal people at Myall Creek in 1838, the colony erupted into a violent rage. The governor, Sir George Gipps, realised it would be unpopular to punish colonists for the slaughter of Aboriginal people. As a result, massacres continued into the twentieth century.

The war between Aboriginal people and settlers is rarely mentioned in Australian history books as the settlers deliberately covered up the massacres and the terrible cruelties inflicted on the Aboriginal people.

In the following chapters you will meet a few of Australia's earliest colonists and European explorers and read from their accounts as they travelled across the continent and claimed the land as their own. Their descriptions and observations are clear evidence of Aboriginal farming and land care, of crops and harvests, of permanent settlements, of houses and communal buildings, of engineering, of fish traps and wells, and of food storage.

OPPOSITE: DETAIL, 'HOMEWARD BOUND', J.T. DOYLE c.1863, SHOWS COLONIAL DROVERS HERDING CATTLE
ABOVE: FROM THE SKETCHBOOK *SCENES FROM ABORIGINAL LIFE* BY KWAT KWAT ARTIST TOMMY MCRAE, 1862

TWO AGRICULTURE

SHE SWEPT HER hand through the grass heads at Cuddie Springs. She glanced down at what she had gathered and walked back to her camp wondering.

She looked around, selected two stones and ground the seeds into a powder.

She probably tasted it and later that day she mixed it with a little water and cooked it by the fire.

She made bread.

That was 65,000 years ago. The next people to try to bake bread were the Egyptians 13,000 years later. That woman came up with an idea far more important to humankind than the moon landing. That's genius, isn't it?

Are we guessing that it was a woman? Of course. But Aboriginal culture tells us that the grindstone was the responsibility of women way back in ancestral time so to credit a woman with the science is logical.

● ● ●

OPPOSITE: GRINDING WELL AND SHARPENING GROOVES, CATTAI, NEW SOUTH WALES
LEFT: YAM DAISY AND TUBER

WESTERN AUSTRALIA

Lieutenant Grey might have been the worst explorer on earth, but he was wealthy enough to choose his own career. He was the first European explorer to travel into many parts of Western Australia, but his 1839 trip to the Kimberley was a disaster.

On his ocean journey to the north of Western Australia, the whale boats, over-loaded and ill-designed for the assignment, were wrecked on the beach at Gantheaume Bay and all provisions were lost. Grey and his party were forced to walk back to Perth.

Despite the terrible predicament, Grey recorded all that he saw:

And as we wound along the native path my wonder augmented; the path increased in breadth and its beaten appearance, whilst along the side we found frequent wells, some of which were ten and twelve feet [3–4 metres] deep, and were altogether executed in a superior manner. We now crossed the dry bed of a stream, and from that emerged upon a tract of light fertile soil quite overrun with warran plants [the yam plant, Dioscorea hastifolia*] the root of which is a favourite article of food with the natives. This was the first time we had seen this plant on our journey and now for three and a half consecutive*

OPPOSITE: YAM SEED HEAD
RIGHT: HARVESTED YAM TUBER

miles [5.6 kilometres] traversed a piece of land, literally perforated with holes the natives made to dig this root; indeed we could with difficulty walk across it on that account whilst the tract extended east and west as far as we could see … more had been done to secure provision from the ground by hard manual labour than I could believe it in the power of uncivilized man to accomplish. After crossing a low limestone range we came upon another equally fertile warran ground … and (next day) passed two native villages, or as the men termed them, towns – the huts of which they composed differed from those in the southern districts, in being built, and very nicely plastered over the outside with clay, and clods of turf, so that although now uninhabited they were evidently intended for fixed places of residence.

Source: Grey quoted in Gerritsen, R. (2008)

Grey is describing permanent houses, human-made wells, planted fields of yam – in other words an organised settlement surrounded by the crops of managed farmland.

● ● ●

OPPOSITE: MATURE YAM TUBERS

Native women getting Tam,bourn roots
27 Aug 1835

VICTORIA

When John Batman's party first landed at Indented Head in Victoria, or Port Phillip District as it was known, in June 1835, he left Andrew Todd to guard the stores. Todd passed the long days by talking to the Wathaurong people and sketching.

One of his sketches shows a line of women digging for yam daisy tubers or murrnong (*Microseris lanceolata*), the sweet little potato that was a staple vegetable of Aboriginal people's diet. The area the women were working was clear of other plants because they had been harvesting and propagating the area for thousands of years.

The Chief Aboriginal Protector of the Port Phillip District, George Augustus Robinson, recorded in 1841:

> *the native women were spread out over the plain as far as the eye could see, collecting Murnong, or in this language pannin, a privilege they would not be permitted except under my protection. I inspected their bags and baskets on return and each had a load as much as she could carry.*
>
> *Source:* Robinson, G.A. (1998)

OPPOSITE: DETAIL, YAM DIGGERS AT INDENTED HEAD, VICTORIA, 1835. YAMS WERE A STAPLE OF THE FIRST PEOPLES' DIET

Like Lieutenant Grey in Western Australia, Robinson is describing the harvest of a cultivated crop. His diaries go on to record the pressures on the Aboriginal diet after colonisation as the settlers forced Aboriginal people from their cultivated fields and prevented them from harvesting the crops.

In 1836 in Sunbury, Victoria, it was observed that Aboriginal people had worked their gardens so well and for so long that large earthen mounds had been created. The process of weeding and harvesting, and the Aboriginal knowledge of contouring land for erosion protection, had created low embankments around the flanks of the hillsides.

One of the earliest English farmers near Melbourne in Victoria, Isaac Batey, was amazed by the agricultural methods of the Aboriginal people and the productivity they had created. He recorded:

> *the soil (on a sloping ridge) is rich in basaltic clay, evidently well fitted for the production of myrnongs [*Microseris lanceolata*]. On the spot are numerous mounds with short spaces between each, and as all these are at right angles to the ridge's slope it is conclusive evidence that they were the work of human hands extending over a long series of years.*

Source: Batey quoted in Frankel, D. (1982)

OPPOSITE: DETAIL, 'GISBORNE HILL', 1875, SHOWS THE CLEAR FIELDS OF WHICH THE ENGLISH SETTLERS WERE ABLE TO TAKE ADVANTAGE

LEFT: FROM THE SKETCHBOOK *SCENES FROM ABORIGINAL LIFE* BY KWAT KWAT ARTIST TOMMY MCRAE, 1862

ABORIGINAL GRAIN BELT
CONTEMPORARY GRAIN BELT

This soil preparation, known as terracing, was also recorded by other colonists. Apart from the benefits to the soil of continuous tilling, the terraces captured the run-off as it flowed down the gentle slope after rain. This is a technique that any modern farmer would recognise as good soil management.

Batey also remembered the women harvesting and washing the tubers in vast quantities. But soon after his arrival in 1846 he wrote:

Where once abundant they have become quite extinct ... Elsewhere it has been intimated that our domestic animals had eaten them out, yet there was another factor of destruction in the soil becoming hardened with the continuous tramping of sheep, cattle or horses.

Another farmer from Sunbury, Edward Page, supported Batey's observations:

Mr Edward Page said, 'When we first came here I started a vegetable garden, the soil dug like ashes.' It has to be added it was a spot free of timber or scrub of any description, the soil a reddish loam of great depth.

● ● ●

OPPOSITE: THE EXPLORERS' EARLY RECORDS ARE SO PERSISTENT IN THEIR DESCRIPTION OF GRAIN HARVESTS FROM ALL PARTS OF THE COUNTRY THAT NORMAN TINDALE WAS ABLE TO CREATE A MAP OF AUSTRALIA SHOWING WHERE ABORIGINAL PEOPLE HARVESTED GRAIN AS COMPARED TO WHERE GRAIN HAS BEEN HARVESTED SINCE WHITE SETTLEMENT

The introduction of sheep had a devastating effect on Aboriginal land and crops. When ships unloaded their cargo of sheep at port, the sheep walked away from the shore and found the Aboriginal crops of murrnong, vanilla lilies, orchids and cress. Because a sheep's teeth allows it to eat plants right to the ground, they destroyed the indigenous crops.

As colonists staked their claims on the most productive Aboriginal land, their sheep ate their way across Australia, destroying in just a few seasons soil that had been carefully cultivated for thousands of years.

As well as yams, Aboriginal people farmed a variety of native grasses for grain. Like wheat, these grains would be ground into flour and used to make pastes or bread.

Native grasses grew mainly in dry inland areas and were so important to some Aboriginal groups that they called themselves 'grass people'.

An Aboriginal man, Walter Smith, worked with camels in Central Australia throughout much of the last century, and saw how the locals planted grass seeds:

They chuck a bit there ... Not much, you know, wouldn't be a handful ...

one seed there, one seed there … [of] course they chuck a little bit of dirt on, not too much though. And soon as first rain comes … it will grow then.

Source: Smith quoted in Kimber, R.G. (1984)

Once the rain came, mainly over the warmer months, grass would begin to grow and spread. When it was tall, the local people would gather the grass and collect the grain.

Explorer Thomas Mitchell was a Scot and a great bushman. He was a hothead, so hot he fought the last duel in Australia but succeeded only in shooting a hole in his opponent's hat. He was also a poet, artist, surveyor, town planner and a prolific writer.

In 1832, Mitchell was exploring the Barwon River region of Queensland when he came across substantial crops of the wheat-like grain *Panicum laevinode*. In his diary he wrote:

the grass is pulled … and piled in hayricks, so that the aspect of the desert was softened into the agreeable semblance of a hay-field … we found the ricks or hay-cocks extending for miles.

Source: Mitchell, T.L. (1839)

Later he found yet another plain where:

the seed is made by the natives into a kind of paste or bread. Dry heaps of this grass, that had been pulled expressly for this purpose of gathering the seed, lay along our path for many miles.

Source: Mitchell (1839)

These journal entries are further evidence that Aboriginal people were farming – in this instance cultivating and harvesting pastures of grain. Researchers estimate there were over 140 grasses harvested by Aboriginal people.

Mitchell travelled through the volcanic plains of western Victoria in 1832. He wrote in his journal:

We crossed a beautiful plain … ornamented with trees, which, although dropt in nature's careless haste, gave the country the appearance of an extensive park.

But the beautiful plains were not, as Mitchell describes, an accident of God. They were the result of Aboriginal people farming the land for thousands of years.

Eric Rolls reported settlers and surveyors near the Hunter River commenting that:

the hills have a look of a park and Grounds laid out.

Source: Rolls, E. (1981)

OPPOSITE: KANGAROO GRASS

Early colonial artists also recorded cultivated fields in their paintings and drawings. Historians assumed that in their depictions of open fields and pasture, the artists were romanticising the Australian landscape, and calling on their memories of the English countryside. But these paintings, showing cleared fields of pasture, were accurate to the landscape the artists would have seen. The artists were recording Aboriginal farmland.

Aboriginal farming would have looked very different to farming in England. Aboriginal people grew crops that were native to Australia and used tools and techniques suited to this environment. But despite the crops and the tools being unfamiliar, the process was the same – selecting seeds to plant, preparing the soil, harvesting the crops and storing the produce.

OPPOSITE: DETAIL, 'CONSTITUTION HILL AT SUNSET, VAN DEIMEN'S LAND', BY JOHN GLOVER 1840, SHOWING BEAUTIFUL PLAINS ORNAMENTED WITH TREES, SUCH AS MITCHELL DESCRIBES IN HIS DIARIES

THREE AQUACULTURE

AQUACULTURE IS THE farming of fish and other water animals for food. This was established all over Australia thousands of years before the first colonists arrived.

BREWARRINA

The Brewarrina fish traps are strong – strong enough to survive floods. They have always been there. They were designed in such a way that all families could receive enough fish but sufficient numbers could pass through the traps to breed further upstream. Everyone can have their share and the fish can also prosper. The Brewarrina fishing system in north-west New South Wales is one example of a large-scale fishing operation.

The fish-trap system is so old that the local Aboriginal people, the Ngemba, say it was constructed by the creator spirit Baiame. There are differing opinions as to its age. An archaeological team calculated the age of the fish traps to be at least 40,000 years. Some archaeologists claim the Brewarrina traps are the oldest human construction on earth. By whatever measure, they rank as some of humankind's earliest constructions.

OPPOSITE: FISH TRAPS, BREWARRINA, NEW SOUTH WALES. PARTICULAR FAMILIES MANAGED AND USED PARTICULAR PONDS IN THE SYSTEM

LEFT: FROM THE SKETCHBOOK *SCENES FROM ABORIGINAL LIFE* BY KWAT KWAT ARTIST TOMMY MCRAE, 1862

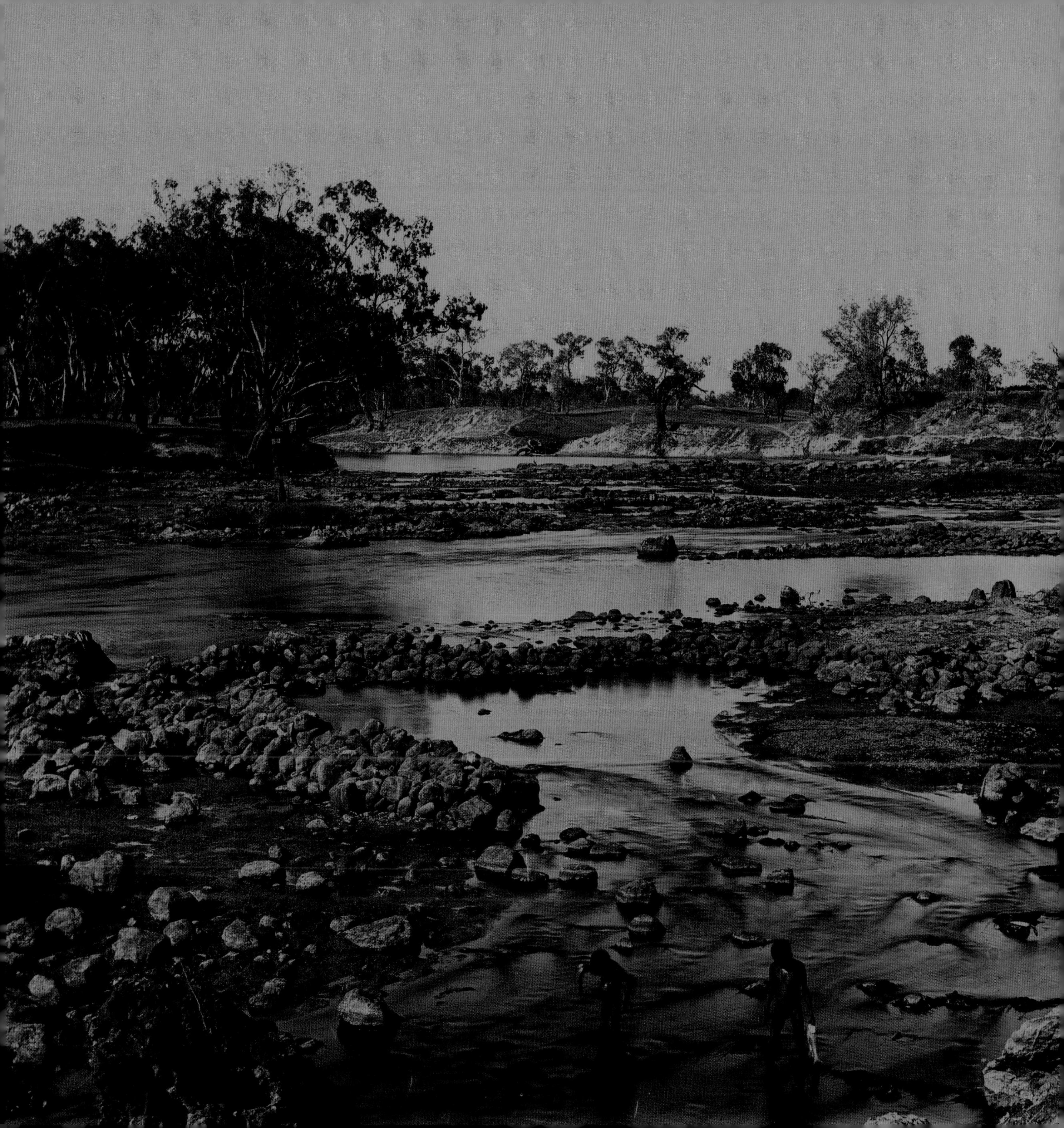

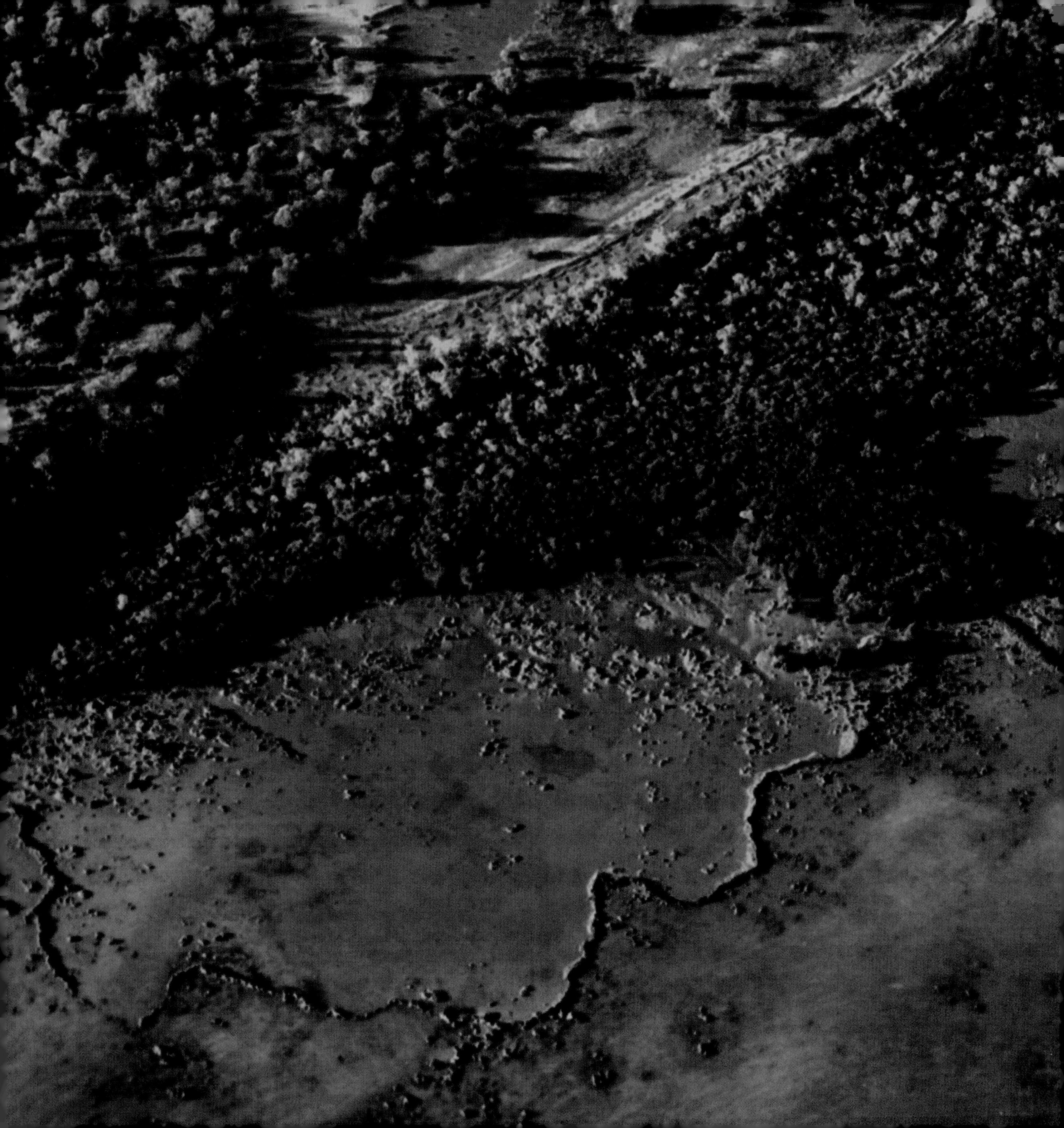

Witnesses in the 1800s who saw the system in operation were astounded by the efficiency of the traps and the enormous harvest of fish. They also remarked on the careful effort Aboriginal clans took to maintain breeding stock. The traps were designed to allow breeding stock to pass through so that upstream fisheries could have their share.

The engineering of the structure was ingenious. A system of locking the boulders in place fixed the trap to the bed of the stream. Observers were amazed that the traps were secure enough to withstand regular floods.

The Brewarrina trap is only one of hundreds of such systems that were built across the continent. Large numbers of people depended on fishing traps along most inland rivers.

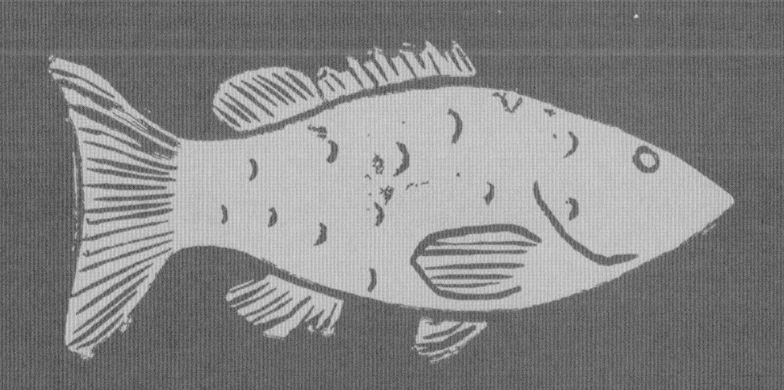

OPPOSITE: DETAIL, WELLESLEY ISLAND FISH TRAPS

THIS PAGE: PERCH

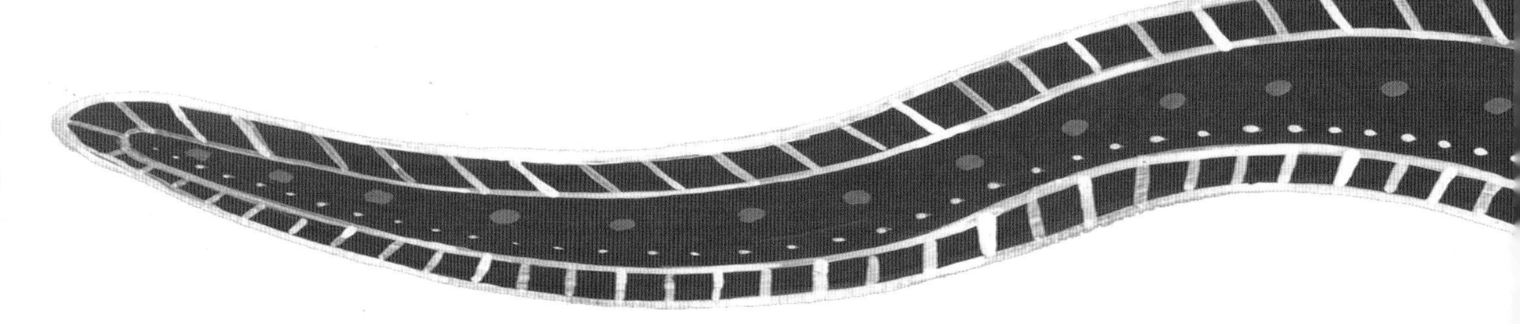

MURRAY RIVER

Young and seeking adventure, James Kirby and Peter Beveridge were two of the first Europeans to visit the Murray River in 1843.

On the orders of Beveridge's father, the pair drove 1,000 head of cattle from Beveridge's Melbourne property to set up a new estate on the Murray River. One morning, as they walked along the river, they came across a group of Aboriginal people. Beveridge wrote in his diary that:

> *[M]any of them had green boughs in their hands, and after 'yabber yabber' they began swinging the boughs over and round their heads, and shouting 'Cum-a-thunga, cum-a-thunga.' We of course did not know what their meaning was by these antics, but we guessed that by it they meant we were welcome to their land, and we made them understand that we were highly pleased at their antics and quite delighted at the words 'cum-a-thunga' … three or four of them jumped into the water, and swam across and gave us a lot more 'cum-a-thunga', so much so that they almost made themselves hoarse with shouting 'cum-a-thunga'.*

Source: Beveridge quoted in Kirby, J. (1897)

ABOVE: EEL

Linguists of the Wati Wati and neighbouring Wemba Wemba language reveal a phrase, 'cum.mar.ca.ta.ca', recorded by the Aboriginal Protector, George Augustus Robinson. Its probable meaning is 'Get up and go away'.

As Beveridge describes, the Aboriginal men repeated this phrase until they were hoarse. It is very unlikely that they were inviting Kirby and Beveridge to take their land.

In the following days, Beveridge and Kirby observed substantial weirs built all through the river system and speculated on who might have created them. As they were the first Europeans in the area, they reluctantly conceded that these weirs were probably built by Aboriginal people.

When Beveridge and Kirby witnessed people fishing with canoes, lines and nets, the purpose of the weirs was revealed. Aboriginal people had dammed the streams behind earthen platforms to create the weirs. Channels flowed into these large constructions to direct fish.

On one particular day Kirby noticed a man by one of these weirs. He wrote:

a black would sit near the opening and just behind him a tough stick about ten feet [3 metres] long was stuck in the ground with the thick end down. To the thin end of this rod was attached a line with a noose at the other end; a wooden peg was fixed under the water at the opening in the fence to which this noose was caught, and when the fish made a dart to go through the opening he was caught by the gills, his force undid the loop from the peg, and the spring of the stick threw the fish over the head of the black, who would then in a most lazy manner reach back his hand, undo the fish, and set the loop again around the peg.

Rather than acknowledging the ingenuity of this automatic fishing machine, Kirby wrote:

> *I have often heard of the indolence of the blacks and soon came to the conclusion after watching a blackfellow catch fish in such a lazy way, that what I had heard was perfectly true.*

OPPOSITE: SCHOOL OF PERCH
RIGHT: MUSSELS

42 LAKE CONDAH AND OTHER FISH TRAPS

Escaped convict William Buckley visited Lake Condah before 1836. He was amazed at the quantities of fish captured in the traps there. He also reported seeing fish-harvesting systems on smaller streams west of Port Phillip Bay.

As John Batman began his venture into Victoria, he saw fish traps on all the rivers he came across. He admired their ingenuity and noted that the existence of a fish trap meant there would be a permanent village nearby.

Early explorers and colonists observed aquaculture systems in all parts of Australia. These original systems were perfectly adapted for the particular conditions of the area and the species they were intended to catch.

Today very few of these imaginative systems exist. Aboriginal Protector William Thomas, who saw many aquacultural systems, reported that most traps and villages were destroyed by Europeans in the first days after their arrival. One such system belonged to a particularly large village near Port Fairy in Western Victoria. The village had more than 30 houses and was capable of accommodating around 200 to 250 people. Early settlers burnt the whole village and destroyed the fishery sluice gates.

OPPOSITE: QUEENSLAND FISHING SYSTEM

FOUR HOME

BEFORE THE BRITISH claimed Australia as their territory, they declared it *terra nullius* – which means 'land belonging to no one'. Although they knew Aboriginal people lived here, the British argued Australia was not settled because there was no evidence of houses, towns, roads or farms. Britain used this reasoning to claim Australia.

The common perception even today is that Aboriginal Australians were nomadic and lived in impermanent or moveable simple structures, which early settlers named 'humpies'. However, the explorers' diaries and journals are brimming with references to substantial Aboriginal housing across the continent – even those parts of Australia that today we think of as being harsh and difficult to live in.

In his diaries, Thomas Mitchell recorded his astonishment at entire villages of houses.

> *[Some huts] … being large, circular; and made of straight rods meeting at an upright pole in the centre; the outside had first been covered with bark and grass, and the entirety coated over with clay. The fire appeared to have been made nearly in the centre; and a hole at the top had been left as a chimney.*
>
> *Source:* Mitchell, T.L. (1839)

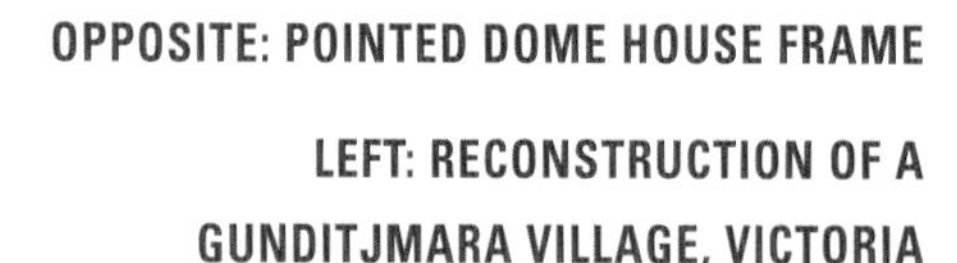

OPPOSITE: POINTED DOME HOUSE FRAME

LEFT: RECONSTRUCTION OF A GUNDITJMARA VILLAGE, VICTORIA

After counting the houses, Mitchell estimated the population as over 1,000 people. He was disappointed that nobody was home – the evidence is that Aboriginal people had lived at this place for a very long time and had only just left.

Mitchell described what we would call a village, which included large huts where people would gather. Some could accommodate up to 50 people.

One of the party commented that the buildings were:

> *of very large dimensions, one capable of containing at least 40 persons and of very superior construction.*
>
> *Source:* Andrews, A.E.J. (1986)

Permanent houses in villages such as these are further evidence of Aboriginal people's dependence on agriculture. Permanent settlements show people are confident in having a reliable and known food source.

In the 1840s, the centre of Australia was still largely unknown to Europeans and efforts to explore it had been prevented and disrupted by the harsh terrain and inhospitable conditions.

Charles Sturt was a good bushman and a great writer. In 1844, he led an expedition to Australia's centre, which was hampered by difficulty. It was so hot that thermometers burst, screws fell out of boxes and the lead fell from pencils. When Sturt's party

OPPOSITE AND THIS PAGE: DOME HOUSE

reached Cooper's Creek, in what is now known as Sturt Stony Desert, they were confronted by sand ridges 30 metres high. They continued, enduring incredible hardships, but Sturt climbed one final dune and peered down onto the plain. His journal records:

> *on gaining the summit [we] were hailed with a deafening shout by 3 or 400 natives, who had assembled on the flat below … The scene was of the most animated description, and was rendered still more striking from the [size] of the native huts, at which there were a number of women and children …*
>
> *Source:* Sturt, C. (1849)

Sturt was looking at a village on the dry floodplain of the Warburton River. Sick and weary and with horses stumbling with hunger, thirst and fatigue, Sturt was amazed to find a large settlement of Aboriginal people in an area in which he thought it was impossible to survive. He was also very lucky.

> *Had these people been of an unfriendly temper, we could not in any possibility have escaped them … but, so far from exhibiting any unkind feeling, they treated us with genuine hospitality, and we might certainly have commanded whatever they had. Several of them brought us large troughs of water, and*

OPPOSITE AND THIS PAGE: ROBINSON'S DRAWING OF CARAMUT, A VILLAGE IN SOUTH-WESTERN VICTORIA, c.1840

Blacks, about 30 Miles N.E. of Port Fairy, by what
[illegible] formed the Spring creek, before settlers came among
them had a Regular Village, my Informant who drew the
[illegible] that there were between 20 & 30 [illegible] some
of them Big enough to hold a dozen People, their shape
[illegible] under an aperture at top to let out smoke, which in
rainy weather they covered with large sod — The Form
like a Beehive about 6 feet high & [illegible] about 10 feet
in diameter an opening about 3 ft 6 in, which they covered
[illegible] at night with piece Bark — These Blacks made regular
[illegible] in creeks to catch Fish — They could make Straw [illegible]
[illegible] Baskets very different — about 1839 settlers [illegible]
[illegible] on this spot — about May 1842 a Station was formed
the opposite side of the creek to this Native Settlement

when we had taken a little, held them up for our horses to drink ... placing the troughs they carried against their breast, they allowed the horses to drink, with their noses almost touching them. They likewise offered us some roasted ducks, and some cake. When we walked over to their camp, they pointed to a large new hut, and told us we could sleep there ... and (later) they brought a quantity of sticks for us to make a fire, wood being extremely scarce.

In later expeditions, Sturt saw buildings in a number of locations including, in 1845, several at Strzelecki Creek. The entrance of one of these structures was 14.5 metres wide and 2 metres high. The roof was plastered with a thick coating of clay.

Sturt wrote about huts made with strong oval arches, covered with boughs and rendered with:

a thick coating of clay so that the huts were impervious to wind and heat. These huts were a considerable size, and close to each there was a smaller one equally well made ... and had apparently been swept prior to the departure of the inhabitants.

OPPOSITE: RECONSTRUCTION OF A GUNDITJMARA VILLAGE, VICTORIA

LEFT: COLONIAL ON HORSEBACK

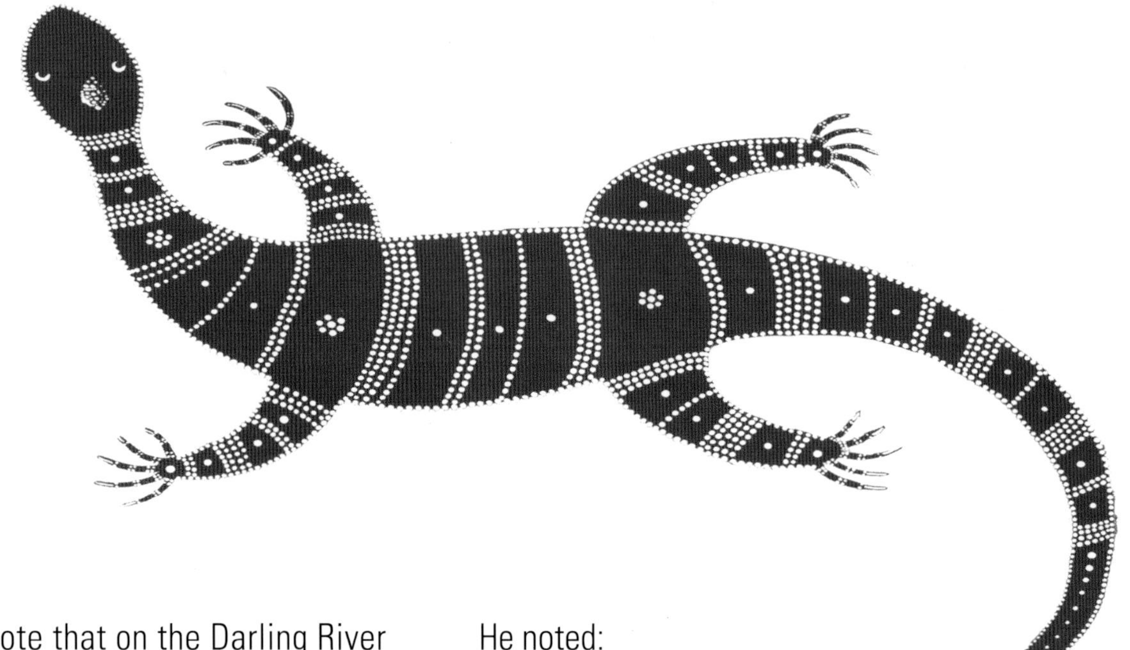

Sturt wrote that on the Darling River in New South Wales the houses:

were made of strong boughs fixed in a circle in the ground, so as to meet in a common centre; on these there was … a thick seam of grass and leaves and over this a compact coating of clay. They were from eight to ten feet [2.4–3 metres] in diameter, and about four and a half feet [1.37 metres] high, the opening into them not being larger than to allow a man to creep in. These huts also faced north-west, and each one had a smaller one attached.

He noted:

these huts were built in rows, the front of one hut being at the back of the other, and it appeared to be a singular but universal custom to erect a smaller hut at no great distance from the large ones.

It became evident that the smaller huts were used for animals, mostly dogs, or the storage of grain and other food.

Even in the harsh and difficult terrain of the desert, Sturt saw Aboriginal wells and substantial houses. Several villages were

ABOVE AND RIGHT: GOANNA

located near Birdsville – a place Australians mythologise as remote and inhospitable.

It is clear from Sturt's journals that the desert in which he twice nearly died was populated by Aboriginal people, taking advantage of vast plains and managing the seasonal water to plant crops, harvest grain and successfully store it. The desert was a productive and healthy environment for large numbers of Aboriginal people.

On the Darling River, explorers reported similar villages to those described by Sturt and Mitchell and estimated the population of each to be no less than a thousand. Mitchell saw villages comprising large houses on the Barcoo River and added that some had several rooms each. The villages were linked by extensive networks of well-worn paths, many of which have formed the basis for today's highways.

In 1883, the Government Surveyor, David Lindsay, reported from his survey of Arnhem Land that he:

> *came on the site of a large native encampment, quite a quarter of a mile [0.4 kilometres] across. Framework of several large humpies one having been 12 feet [3.6 metres] high: small enclosures as if some small game had been yarded and kept alive … This camp*

must have contained quite 500 natives, and have been the site of some great festival, the corroboree or dancing grounds, being numerous and well worn.

Source: McMillan, A. (2001)

Even in describing what must have been large buildings, David Lindsay still used the word 'humpy'.

Edward Curr admitted that the sophisticated bark huts made by Aboriginal people were easily the most comfortable of any habitations in the colonial bush. At Mallacoota in 1842, Joseph Lingard met two Aboriginal men and:

made bold to go into their retreat, which I found to be like a house inside.

Source: Howe, K.R. (1990)

Historian Rupert Gerritsen lists numerous reports by explorers and early settlers who saw large villages. Mitchell referred to the banks of the Darling where:

the buzz of population gave to the banks at this place the cheerful character of a village in a populous country.

Source: Mitchell, T.L. (1839)

As Gerritsen summarises:

Most Australians would find such comments rather surprising given that much of this area is usually seen as being desolate and inhospitable.

Source: Gerritsen, R. (2008)

But people did live there and prospered, their villages buzzing with happiness, the towns thriving because the inhabitants were utilising the natural conditions and developing the indigenous grains and tubers.

Houses and villages were described in all corners of the country, but the styles were quite diverse. As with any good design, architectural style varied according to the climate and the materials available. Where safe cave systems occurred they were also used for housing and ceremonial purposes, but in general explorers saw houses.

There are hundreds of reports of this kind. Unfortunately the destruction of the houses, like the destruction of grasslands, was rapid.

The remnants of towns are still to be found but firsthand reports of exploration and settlement contain numerous accounts of how substantial villages were burnt, the foundations stolen for other buildings, and the occupants killed by warfare, murder and disease.

It is not surprising that after 1860 most colonists saw no evidence of any prior complex civilisation. Later visitors to the country claimed to see no structure more substantial than a windbreak and no population that was not humiliated, debased and diseased.

Despite the subsequent destruction it is clear from firsthand records that large populations survived in every corner of the land in more comfort than we have been led to believe.

FIVE FOOD STORAGE

THE CLANS GATHER to meet – Manaroo, Bidwell, Ngarigo, Yuen, Thawa, Diringanj, Walbanga, Ngunuwal and more. The moths are plentiful. It is a time to feast and talk. During the harvest of the moths, they are treated carefully. If the body of the moth is scorched during cooking, it is said a great storm will arise and blow the moths off course and out to sea. And the harvest will be lost.

Aboriginal groups stored their harvests, including grains, nuts, fruits, yams, eggs, insects, fish and meat. This meant that as the seasons changed and different foods were ready to harvest, a variety would be available and the people would be protected from a shortage of food.

There were three types of food storage used in Australia by Aboriginal people.

CACHING: Small stores, such as acacia and eucalypt seeds, were preserved and left in a protected location.

The Kukatja and Pintupi of the Great Sandy Desert harvested acacia and eucalyptus seeds, and covered them with spinifex for consumption later in the year when all other foods had been exhausted.

STOCKPILING: This was most commonly used prior to large ceremonies where hundreds of people would gather for an extended period. Examples of stockpiling were seen by many explorers, who often

OPPOSITE AND ABOVE: BOGONG MOTHS

helped themselves to these stores to survive on their expeditions.

DIRECT STORAGE: Aboriginal people made chambers from clay and straw for storing seeds and fruits, nuts, gum, tubers of various sorts, eggs, meat, fish, fish oil and even mussels. Large grain stores of more than 50 kilograms were found in perfect condition sewn up in animal skins. Hollow trees and rock wells were also used.

Many explorers came across Aboriginal food stores, including Arthur Ashwin who found several stockpiles. While travelling through the Barkly Tableland in northern Australia, he found a shelter in a fenced village which:

> *stored 17 large wooden dishes [each more than 1 metre long] filled with grass seed as large as rice.*
>
> *Source:* A.C. Ashwin (1932) in Gerritsen, R. (2008)

Ashwin estimated this was about one ton or 1,016 kilograms of seeds.

Ashwin at times helped himself to the 'delicious grain' he came across, and on one occasion thought that it was:

> *a pity we did not take more.*

His use of this carefully stored grain must have created great hardship for the harvesters.

Skin bags were frequently used to store grain and other produce. Explorer Charles Coxon found 45 kilograms of grain near Castlereagh River.

OPPOSITE AND THIS PAGE: MURRNONG / YAM DAISIES

On his search for Burke and Wills, Alfred Howitt described one of the grain stores he came across:

> *Near Lake Lipson, one of my party found about two bushels contained in a grass case daubed with mud. It looked like a small clay coffin and was concealed ... the munyoura [munyeroo, nardoo] bower tastes like linseed-meal, and is by no means unpleasant when baked in ashes and eaten hot.*
>
> *Source:* Howitt (1855) in Smyth, R.B (1878)

All types of food were preserved and stored. But the preservation and storage of food became more difficult when the clans were forced into constant movement by the advance of pastoralists.

OPPOSITE: BUSH BANANAS
ABOVE: BUSH TOMATOES

SIX FIRE

EUROPEAN SETTLERS saw fire as a threat. Aboriginal people viewed it differently. Many early records describe Aboriginal groups lighting fires to burn areas of land. Most Europeans thought this behaviour was strange or alarming. Some, however, such as settler Edward Curr, realised that burning played an important role in managing the land:

> *there was another instrument in the hands of these savages which must be credited with results which it would be difficult to over-estimate. I refer to the fire-stick; for the blackfellow was constantly setting fire to the grass and trees … he tilled his land and cultivated his pastures with fire.*
>
> *Source:* Curr quoted in Gammage, R. (2011)

Aboriginal people burnt specific areas of land every few years, rotating through different areas from year to year. They timed the burning around particular seasons and weather conditions. This approach controlled the intensity of fires and allowed animals and plants to survive in surrounding areas.

The complex system had several benefits, including adding nutrients to the soil and keeping areas clear for farming. Within days of the fires, fresh green shoots

OPPOSITE: DETAIL, ABORIGINAL FIRE LAND MANAGEMENT, NORTHERN TERRITORY

would sprout. This attracted animals, making it easier for Aboriginal people to hunt.

Aboriginal people learnt over thousands of years how to use fire effectively and safely. Jinoor Jack, an Aboriginal man from East Gippsland, shared his knowledge with emancipated convict Robert Alexander. He told Alexander that every five years in February or March he should burn the land:

> *after the longest day when the sap begins to go down. In that period there are westerly winds in the morning that change to northeast in the afternoon, which provide natural back burn.*
>
> *Source:* O'Conner, N. and K. Jones (2003)

Unfortunately most Europeans did not value Aboriginal knowledge. When Aboriginal people were forced from their lands, and the European settlers used their own farming methods, the effect of these changes was fast and devastating. Thomas Mitchell, who had so enjoyed the park-like plains when he arrived in Australia, wrote in 1848:

> *the omission of the annual periodic burning by natives of the grass and young saplings has already produced in the open forest lands nearest to Sydney thick forests of young trees … Kangaroos are no longer to be seen there, the grass is choked by underwood …*
>
> *Source:* Mitchell quoted in Gott, B. (2005)

ABOVE AND OPPOSITE: BURNT LEAVES

66 SACRED PLACES

Just as most Australian towns have cemeteries and sacred places today, so did Aboriginal villages. According to early records, these were often places of great beauty.

Mitchell came across a cemetery near the Darling River which he sketched and described.

> *The burying-ground was a fairy like spot, in the midst of a scrub of drooping [wattle trees]. It was extensive, and laid out in walks, which were narrow and smooth … and they meandered in gracefully curved lines, amongst the heaps of reddish earth.*
>
> *Source:* Mitchell, T.L. (1839)

Carved and painted trees often featured in these sacred places. In some areas, young trees were laced together, limb over limb, so that they joined as they grew.

An example of this can still be seen at a farm near Ballarat in Victoria. The now old trees have grown together to create oval-shaped openings.

OPPOSITE: DETAIL, CEMETERY AT MILMERIDIEN, NEAR THE DARLING RIVER, BY THOMAS MITCHELL, 1839

68 SUSTAINABLE FUTURES

Australia is a drying continent. Climate change is leading us to look at things in different ways.

Indigenous species of plants and animals are hardy – they are already adapted to the Australian environment. They do not require any more water than the Australian climate supplies, no more fertiliser than our soils already contain and, as they are adapted to Australian pests, they need no pesticides.

These plants are an environmental boon. Apart from the fact that they are perennial with large root masses adapted to dry conditions, they sequester carbon. This means that they capture carbon dioxide before it enters the atmosphere and contributes to climate change. If we dedicated only 5 per cent of our current farming lands to these plants we would go a long way to meeting our carbon emission targets.

OPPOSITE: MURRNONG

These plants are not only good for the environment and our health, but they also teach us a truer history.

When Europeans first began their classification of eras and the peoples of the world, they decided that five things signified the development of agriculture:

- selection of seed
- preparation of the soil
- harvest of the crop
- storage of the surpluses
- permanent housing.

The evidence of explorers and first witnesses is that most Aboriginal Australians were living in an established agricultural society, which was perhaps ahead of many other parts of the world.

The evidence is that Aboriginal people did build houses, did build dams and wells, did sow, irrigate and till the land, and did construct a system of government that generated peace and prosperity. They intervened in the productivity of this country in clever, ingenious, adapted ways.

It is a different way of looking.

OPPOSITE: FROM THE SKETCHBOOK
SCENES FROM ABORIGINAL LIFE
BY KWAT KWAT ARTIST TOMMY MCRAE, 1862

Baiame, the creator Spirit Emu, left the earth after its creation to reside as a dark shape in the Milky Way. The emu is inextricably linked with the wide grasslands of Australia, the landscape managed by Aboriginal people. The fate of the emu, people and grain are locked in step because, for Aboriginal people, the economy and the spirit are inseparable. Europeans stare at the stars, but Aboriginal people also see the spaces in between where the Spirit Emu resides.

OPPOSITE: EMU DREAMING

74 ACKNOWLEDGEMENTS

I am deeply indebted to Rupert Gerritsen for his book *Australia and the Origins of Agriculture* and Bill Gammage for his essay about Aboriginal gardening and farming. Gammage's book *The Biggest Estate on Earth* investigates, in exhaustive detail, the reports of early explorers and settlers, many of whom talked about the 'gentleman's estate' they had chanced upon. Not a wilderness, not a land peopled by wanderers, but a managed landscape created by the enormous labour of a people intent on creating the best possible conditions for food production.

I owe a great debt to my editor, Margaret Whiskin, for her discrimination and encouragement, and for allowing this book to live. Thank you also to Jennet Cole-Adams.

I'm grateful to the ancestors for their ingenious protection of the land. Where else on earth was there a civilisation that lasted more than 80,000 years and depended on both agriculture ... and peace?

BIBLIOGRAPHY

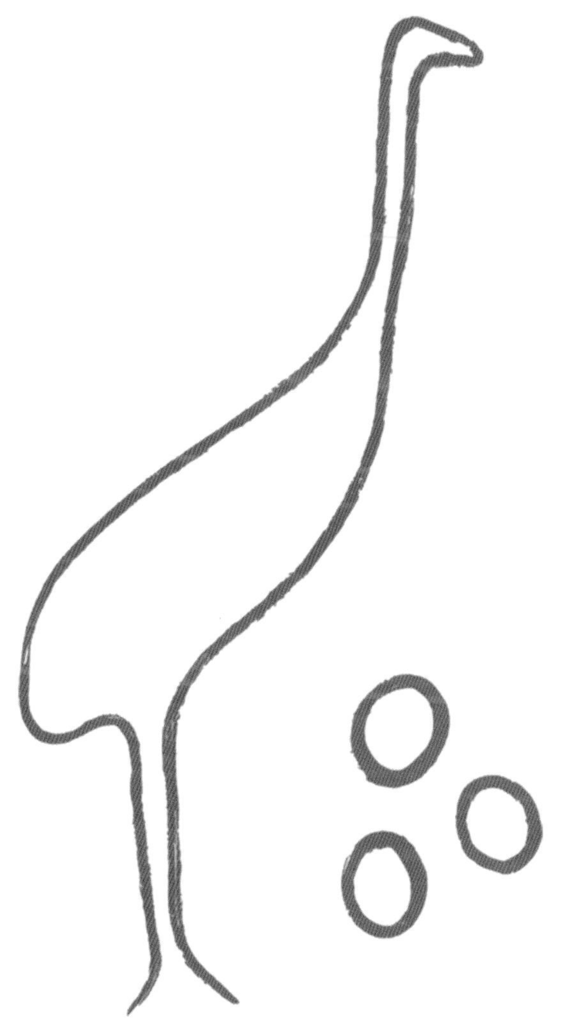

Andrews, A.E.J. (Ed.) *Stapylton with Major Mitchell's Australia Felix Expedition*, Blubber Head Press, Hobart, 1986

Frankel, D. 'An Account of Aboriginal Use of the Yam Daisy', *The Artefact*, vol. 7, nos 1–2, 1982, pp. 43–5

Gammage, B. *The Biggest Estate on Earth*, Allen & Unwin, Sydney, 2011

Gerritsen, R. *Australia and the Origins of Agriculture*, BAR series, Archaeopress, London, 2008

Gott, B. 'Aboriginal Fire Management in S.E. Australia: aims and frequency', *Journal of Biogeography*, no. 32, 2005

Howe, K.R. (Ed.) *Mallacoota Reflections*, Mallacoota and District Historical Society, 1990

Kimber, R.G. *Resource Use and Management in Central Australia*, Australian Aboriginal Studies, Canberra, 1984

Kirby, J. *Old Times in the Bush of Australia: trials and experiences of early bush life in Victoria: during the forties*, G. Robertson and Company, Victoria, 1897

McMillan, A. *An Intruder's Guide to Arnhem Land*, Duffy and Snellgrove, Sydney, 2001

Mitchell, T.L. *Three Expeditions into the Interior of Eastern Australia*, vols 1 and 2, T and W Boone, London, 1839

Mitchell, T.L. *Journal of an Expedition into the Interior of Tropical Australia*, Greenwood Press, New York, 1969

O'Conner, N. and K. Jones *A Journey Through Time*, self-published family history, 2003

Robinson, G.A. *The Journals of George Augustus Robinson*, vol. 2, 31 October 1841, Heritage Matters, Melbourne, 1998

Rolls, E. *A Million Wild Acres*, Nelson, Melbourne, 1981

Smyth, R.B. *The Aborigines of Victoria and the Riverina*, John Ferres, Gvt Printer, Melbourne, 1878

Sturt, C. *Narrative of an Expedition into Central Australia*, T and W Boone, London, 1849

PICTURE CREDITS

PAGE 2: Possum-skin design by the author, Bruce Pascoe. Photograph by Lyn Harwood

PAGE 6: Photograph by Barnaby Norris. From *Emu Dreaming: an introduction to Australian Aboriginal astronomy*, Ray and Cilla Norris, Emu Dreaming, 2009

PAGE 9 / 13 / 14 / 24 / 34 / 71: Details from sketchbook *Scenes from Aboriginal Life* by Kwat Kwat artist Tommy McRae, 1862. State Library of Victoria Pictures Collection

PAGE 11: Detail from John Batman's treaty with the Wurundjeri, 1835. State Library of Victoria

PAGE 12: Detail from 'Conflict on the Rufus, South Australia', published in *The Illustrated Melbourne Post*, 1866. State Library of Victoria

PAGE 15: Detail from 'Homeward Bound' in *Dr Doyle's Sketch Book*, J.T. Doyle & S.T. Gill, c.1862–1863. State Library of Victoria

PAGE 16 / 23 / 33: Yam daisy and tuber drawing by John Conran

PAGE 17: Grinding well and sharpening grooves, Cattai, New South Wales. Photograph by Leanne Mulgo Watson

PAGE 18: Seed head of the yam daisy. Graphic based on photograph by Beth Gott

PAGE 19 / 20: Harvested murrnong tuber. Photograph by Lyn Harwood

PAGE 21: A handful of yams. Photograph by Vicky Shukuroglou

PAGE 22 / 29: 'J.H.W. Native women getting tam bourn roots 27 August 1835', illustration by J.H. Wedge. From the *Todd Journal Andrew (alias William) Todd John Batman's recorder and his Indented Head journal 1985.* La Trobe section, State Library of Victoria

PAGE 25: Detail from 'Gisborne Hill', engraver Samuel Calvert from a drawing by Abram-Louis Buvelot. State Library of Victoria

PAGE 26: 'Perennial Grain Crops for High Water Use — the case for Microlaena stipoides', C.L. Davies, D.L. Waugh and E.C. Lefroy, RIRDC publication number 05/024. Adapted from the *Tindale Map, Aboriginal Tribes of Australia: their terrain, environmental controls, distribution, limits and proper names*, Australian National University Press, Canberra, 1974

Graphic composed of © textures created by Rowena Morgan and Leanne Mulgo Watson

PAGE 31: Kangaroo grass. Graphic based on photograph by Lyn Harwood

PAGE 32: Detail from 'Constitution Hill at Sunset, Van Dieman's Land, from near Mrs Ranson's Public House June 29th 1840', John Glover. La Trobe Picture Collection, State Library of Victoria

PAGE 35: Fishing in the Brewarrina fish traps. Powerhouse Museum

PAGE 36: Wellesley Island fish traps. Photograph by Connah & Jones, University of New England

PAGE 37: Perch by Rowena Morgan

PAGE 38 / 39: Bara (Eel) by Leanne Mulgo Watson

PAGE 40: School of Perch by Rowena Morgan

PAGE 41: Mussels by Rowena Morgan

PAGE 42: Fish by Leanne Mulgo Watson

PAGE 43: Queensland fishing system. Based on a photograph by D.F. Thomson. Drawing by Leanne Mulgo Watson

PAGE 44 / 55: A reconstruction of a Gunditjmara village, western Victoria, by Paul Memmott

PAGE 45: Pointed dome house frame. Photograph from Queensland Museum. Reproduced in Memmott, P. *Gunyah, Goondie and Wurley: the Aboriginal architecture of Australia*, UQP, 2007. Photograph by Lyn Harwood

PAGE 46 / 47: Dome house. Photograph from Queensland Museum. Reproduced in Memmott. P. *Gunyah, Goondie and Wurley. The Aboriginal Architecture of Australia*, UQP, 2007 Photograph by Lyn Harwood

PAGE 48 / 49: Robinson's drawing of Caramut, a village in south-western Victoria, c.1840. From Smyth papers, La Trobe Library, Melbourne. Reproduced in Memmott, *Gunyah, Goondie and Wurley*

PAGE 50: Colonial on horseback. Artist unknown. Private collection.

PAGE 51: Graphic based on reconstruction of a Gunditjmara village, western Victoria, by Paul Memmott.

PAGE 52 / 53: Wirriga (Goanna) by Leanne Mulgo Watson

PAGE 54 / 55: Dry Earth by Leanne Mulgo Watson

PAGE 56 / 57: Bogong Moths by Rowena Morgan

PAGE 58 / 59: Yam Daisies by Rowena Morgan

PAGE 60: Bush Tomatoes by Rowena Morgan

PAGE 61: Bush Bananas by Rowena Morgan

PAGE 63: Aboriginal fire land management. Photograph by Donna Rawlins

PAGE 64 / 65: Burnt Leaves by Leanne Mulgo Watson

PAGE 67: Detail of engraving from Thomas Mitchell's drawing of the cemetery at Milmeridien, near the Darling River, 1839. National Library of Australia

PAGE 69: Murrnong photograph by Lyn Harwood

PAGE 72: Mariong (Emu) Constellation by Leanne Mulgo Watson

PAGE 75: Mariong (Emu) and Eggs by Leanne Mulgo Watson

PAGE 77: Emu by Rowena Morgan

PAGE 79: Eucalypt by Leanne Mulgo Watson

PAGE 80: Author photograph by Matthew Newton, Rummin Productions

INDEX

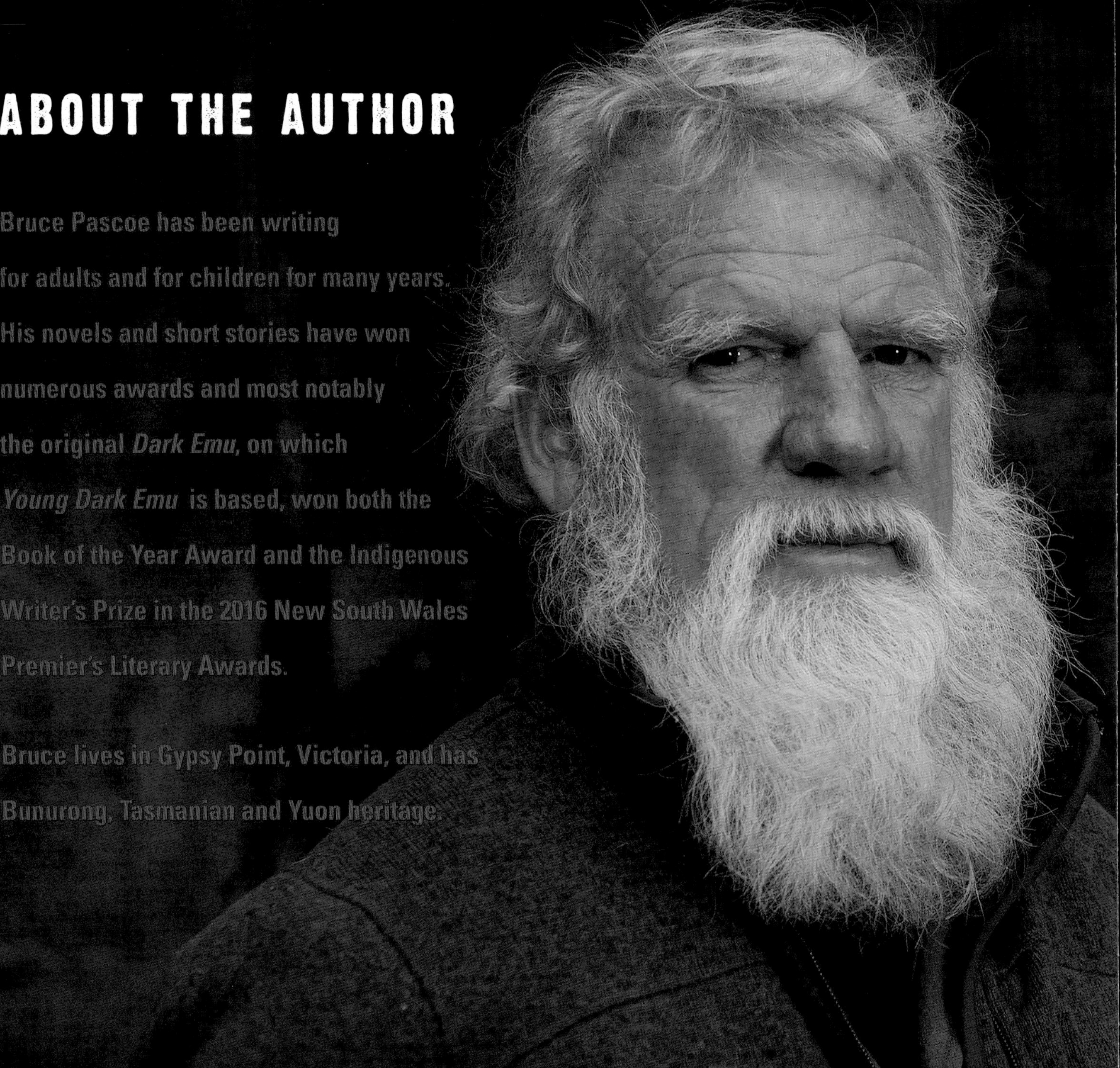

ABOUT THE AUTHOR

Bruce Pascoe has been writing for adults and for children for many years. His novels and short stories have won numerous awards and most notably the original *Dark Emu*, on which *Young Dark Emu* is based, won both the Book of the Year Award and the Indigenous Writer's Prize in the 2016 New South Wales Premier's Literary Awards.

Bruce lives in Gypsy Point, Victoria, and has Bunurong, Tasmanian and Yuon heritage.